LARKS
WITH
SHARKS

A WORLD BOOK DAY
PO   OK

Tim Archbold

**MACMILLAN
CHILDREN'S BOOKS**

First published 1998
by Macmillan Children's Books
a division of Macmillan Publishers Ltd
25 Eccleston Place, London SW1W 9NF
and Basingstoke

Associated companies throughout the world

ISBN 0 330 37036 7

7 9 8 6

A CIP catalogue record for this book is available from the British Library.

Printed and bound in Great Britain by Mackays of Chatham plc, Chatham, Kent.

LARKS
WITH
SHARKS

A WORLD BOOK DAY POETRY BOOK

from Macmillan

THE SECRET LIVES OF TEACHERS
Poems chosen by Brian Moses

PARENT-FREE ZONE
Poems chosen by Brian Moses

ALIENS STOLE MY UNDERPANTS
Poems chosen by Brian Moses

'ERE WE GO!
Football Poems
chosen by David Orme

WE WAS ROBBED
Yet More Football Poems
chosen by David Orme

NOTHING TASTES QUITE LIKE A GERBIL
and other Vile Verses
chosen by David Orme

DRAGONS EVERYWHERE
Poems by Nick Toczek

Contents

Poetry Jump-up

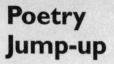

Tell me if Ah seeing right
Take a look down de street

Words dancin
words dancin
till dey sweat
words like fishes
jumpin out a net
words wild and free
joinin de poetry revelry
words back to back
words belly to belly

Come on everybody
come and join de poetry band
dis is poetry carnival
dis is poetry bacchanal
when inspiration call
take yu pen in yu hand
if yu don't have a pen
take yu pencil in yu hand
if yu don't have a pencil
what the hell
so long as de feeling start to swell
just shout de poem out

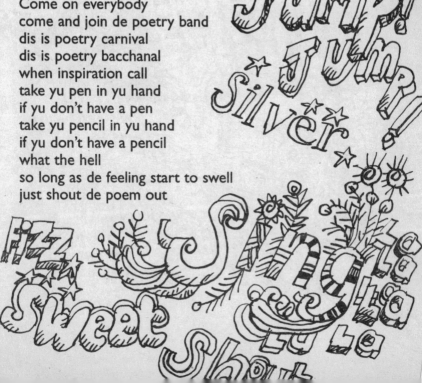

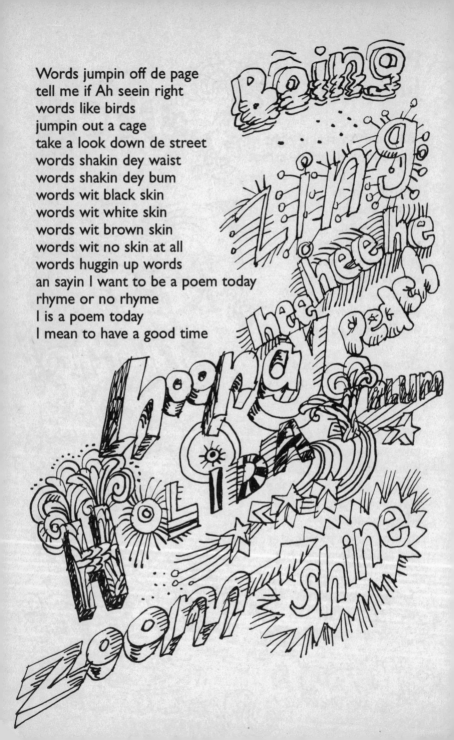

Words jumpin off de page
tell me if Ah seein right
words like birds
jumpin out a cage
take a look down de street
words shakin dey waist
words shakin dey bum
words wit black skin
words wit white skin
words wit brown skin
words wit no skin at all
words huggin up words
an sayin I want to be a poem today
rhyme or no rhyme
I is a poem today
I mean to have a good time

Words feelin hot hot hot
big words feelin hot hot hot
lil words feelin hot hot hot
even sad words can't help
tappin dey toe
to de riddum of de poetry band

Dis is poetry carnival
dis is poetry bacchanal
so come on everybody
join de celebration
all yu need is plenty perspiration
an a little inspiration
plenty perspiration
an a little inspiration

John Agard

9

At Home, Abroad

All summer
I dream of
places I've never
been
where I might
see faces
I've never seen,
like the dark
face of my
father in
Nigeria,
or the pale
face of my
mother in
the Highlands,
or the bright
faces of my
cousins at
Land's End.

All summer
I spell the names
of tricky countries
just in case
I get a sudden
invite: Madagascar,
Cameroon. I draw
cartoons of
airports, big and small.
Who will meet me?
Will they
shake hands or
kiss both cheeks?
I draw
duty frees
with every
country's favourite
sweetie, smiling
a sugary welcome,
and myself,
cap-peaked,
wondering if I am
'home'.

Jackie Kay

Barry's Budgie . . . Beware!

Dave's got a dog the size of a lion
Half-wolf, half-mad, frothing with venom
It chews up policemen and then spits them out
But it's nothing to the bird I'm talking about.

Claire's got a cat as wild as a cheetah
Scratching and hissing, draws blood by the litre
Jumps high walls and hedges, fights wolves on its own
But there's one tough budgie it leaves well alone.

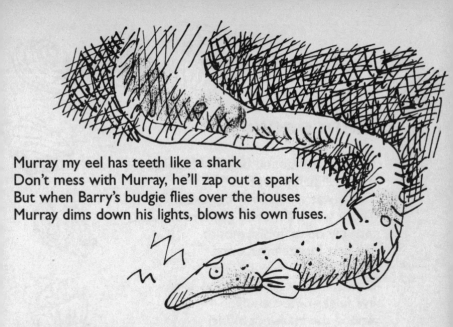

Murray my eel has teeth like a shark
Don't mess with Murray, he'll zap out a spark
But when Barry's budgie flies over the houses
Murray dims down his lights, blows his own fuses.

This budgie's fierce, a scar down its cheek
Tattoos on its wings, a knife in its beak
Squawks wicked words, does things scarcely legal
Someone should tell Barry it's really an eagle.

David Harmer

Chocoholic

Into the half-pound box of Moonlight
my small hand crept.
There was an electrifying rustle.
There was a dark and glamorous scent.
Into my open, moist mouth
the first Montelimar went.

Down in the crinkly second layer,
five finger-piglets snuffled
among the Hazelnut Whirl,
the Caramel Square,
the Black Cherry and Almond Truffle.

Bliss.

I chomped. I gorged.
I stuffed my face,
till only the Coffee Cream
was left for the owner of the box –
tough luck, Anne Pope –
oh, and half an Orange Supreme.

Carol-Ann Duffy

At the End of a School Day

It is the end of a school day
     and down the long drive
come bag-swinging, shouting children.
     Deafened, the sky winces.
       The sun gapes in surprise.

Suddenly the runners skid to a stop,
     stand still and stare
at a small hedgehog
     curled up on the tarmac
       like an old, frayed cricket ball.

A girl dumps her bag, tiptoes forward
        and gingerly, so gingerly
carries the creature
        to the safety of a shady hedge.
            Then steps back, watching.

Girl, children, sky and sun
        hold their breath.
There is a silence,
        a moment to remember
            on this warm afternoon in June.

Wes Magee

My Dog

My dog belongs to no known breed,
A bit of this and that.
His head looks like a small haystack.
He's lazy, smelly, fat.

If I say 'Sit' he walks away.
When I throw a stick or ball
He flops down in the grass as if
He had no legs at all,

And looks at me with eyes that say,
'You threw the thing, not me.
You want it back, then get it back.
Fair's fair you must agree.'

He is a thief. Last week but one
He stole the Sunday Roast.
And showed no guilt at all as we
Sat down to beans on toast.

The only time I saw him run –
And he went like a flash –
Was when a mugger in the park
Tried to steal my cash.

My loyal brave companion flew
Like a missile to the gate
And didn't stop till safely home.
He left me to my fate.

And would I swap him for a dog
Obedient, clean and good,
An honest, faithful, lively chap?
Oh boy, I would! I would!

Vernon Scannell

Den to Let

To let
One self-contained
Detached den.
Accommodation is compact
Measuring one yard square.
Ideal for two eight-year-olds
Plus one small dog
Or two cats
Or six gerbils.
Accommodation consists of:
One living-room
Which doubles as kitchen
Bedroom
Entrance-hall
Dining-room
Dungeon
Space capsule
Pirate boat
Covered wagon
Racing car
Palace
Aeroplane
Junk-room
And lookout post.

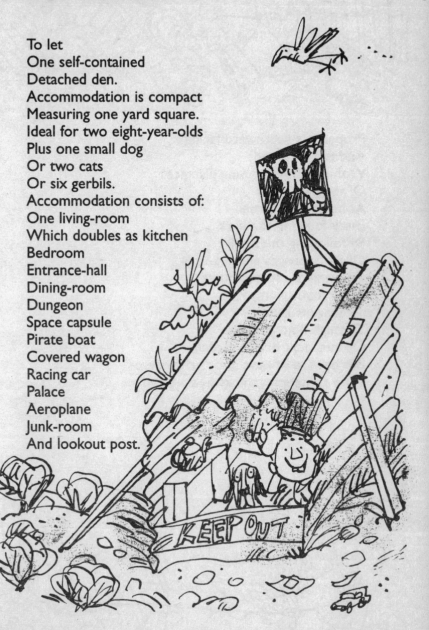

Property is southward facing
And can be found
Within a short walking distance
Of the back door
At bottom of garden.
Easily found in the dark
By following the smell
Of old cabbages and tea-bags.
Convenient escape routes
Past rubbish dump
To Seager's Lane
Through hole in hedge,
Or into next door's garden;
But beware of next door's rhinoceros
Who sometimes thinks he's a poodle.

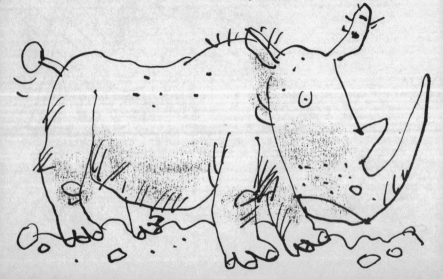

Construction is of
Sound corrugated iron
And roof doubles as shower
During rainy weather.
Being partially underground,
Den makes
A particularly effective hiding place
When in a state of war
With older sisters
Brothers
Angry neighbours
Or when you simply want to be alone.
Some repair work needed
To north wall
Where Mr Spence's foot came through
When planting turnips last Thursday.

With den go all contents
Including:
One carpet – very smelly
One teapot – cracked
One woolly penguin –
No beak and only one wing
One unopened tin
Of sultana pud
One hundred and three Beanos
Dated 1983–1985
And four Rupert annuals.
Rent is free
The only payment being
That the new occupant
Should care for the den
In the manner to which it has been accustomed
And on long Summer evenings
Heroic songs of days gone by
Should be loudly sung
So that old and glorious days
Will never be forgotten.

Gareth Owen

Match of the Year

I am delivered to the stadium by chauffeur-driven
    limousine.
Gran and Grandpa give me a lift in their Mini.

I change into my sparkling clean world-famous designer
    strip.
*I put on my brother's shorts and the T-shirt with tomato
    ketchup stains.*

I give my lightweight professional boots a final shine.
I rub the mud off my trainers.

The coach gives me a final world of encouragement.
Dave, the sports master, tells me to get a move on.

I jog calmly through the tunnel out into the stadium.
I walk nervously onto the windy sports field.

The crowd roars.
Gran and Grandpa shout 'There's our Jimmy!'

The captain talks last-minute tactics.
'Pass to me or I'll belt you.'

The whistle goes. The well-oiled machine goes into
    action.
Where did the ball go?

I pass it skilfully to our international star, Bernicci.
*I kick it away. Luckily, Big Bernard stops it before it
    goes over the line.*

A free kick is awarded to the visiting Premier team. I'm
    part of the impregnable defence.
*The bloke taking the kick looks six feet tall – and just
    as wide . . .*

I stop the ball with a well-timed leap and head it
    expertly up the field.
The ball thwacks me on the head.

The crowd shouts my name! 'Jim-meee! Jim-meee!
    Jim-meee!'
Gran says, 'Eee, our Jim's fallen over.'

    I don't remember any more.

Trevor Millum

Aliens Stole My Underpants

To understand the ways
of alien beings is hard,
and I've never worked it out
why they landed in my backyard.

And I've always wondered why
on their journey from the stars,
these aliens stole my underpants
and took them back to Mars.

They came on a Monday night
when the weekend wash had been done,
pegged out on the line
to be dried by the morning sun.

Mrs Driver from next door
was a witness at the scene
when aliens snatched my underpants –
I'm glad that they were clean!

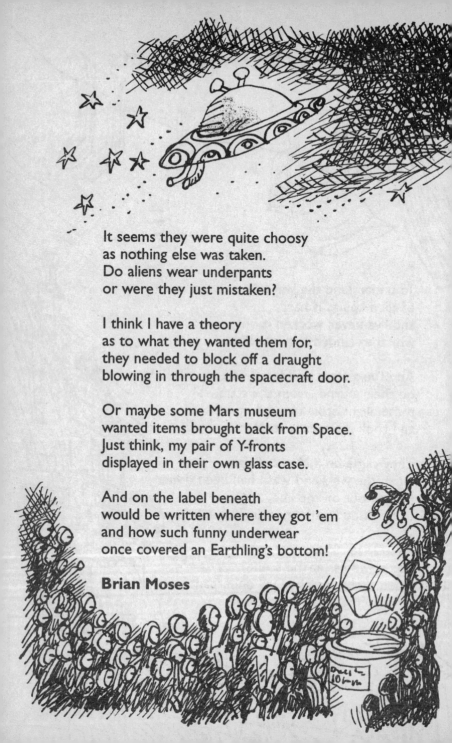

It seems they were quite choosy
as nothing else was taken.
Do aliens wear underpants
or were they just mistaken?

I think I have a theory
as to what they wanted them for,
they needed to block off a draught
blowing in through the spacecraft door.

Or maybe some Mars museum
wanted items brought back from Space.
Just think, my pair of Y-fronts
displayed in their own glass case.

And on the label beneath
would be written where they got 'em
and how such funny underwear
once covered an Earthling's bottom!

Brian Moses

A Good Poem

I like a good poem.
One with lots of fighting
in it. Blood, and the
clanging of armour. Poems

against Scotland are good,
and poems that defeat
the French with crossbows.
I don't like poems that

aren't about anything.
Sonnets are wet and
a waste of time.
Also poems that don't

know how to rhyme.
If I was a poem
I'd play football and
get picked for England.

Roger McGough

Sir's a Secret Agent

Sir's a secret agent
He's licensed to thrill
At Double-Oh Sevening
He's got bags of skill.

He's tall, dark and handsome
With a muscular frame
Teaching's his profession
But Danger's his game!

He's cool and he's calm
When he makes a decision
He's a pilot, sky-diver
And can teach long-division.

No mission's too big
No mission's too small
School-kids, mad scientists
He takes care of them all.

He sorts out the villains
The spies and the crooks
Then comes back to school
And marks all our books!

Tony Langham

Dear Mum

While you were out
A cup went and broke itself on purpose.
A crack appeared in that old blue vase your great granddad
Got from Mr Ming.
Somehow without me even turning on the tap
The sink mysteriously overflowed.
A strange jam-stain,about the size of my hand,
Suddenly appeared on the kitchen wall.
I don't think we'll ever discover exactly how the cat
Managed to turn on the washing machine
(Specially from the inside)
Or how Sis's pet rabbit went and mistook
The waste-disposal unit for a burrow.
I can tell you, I was really scared when, as if by magic,
A series of muddy footprints appeared on your new white
        carpet.
Also, I know the canary looks grubby,
But it took ages and ages
Getting it out the vacuum-cleaner
I was being good (honest)
But I think the house is haunted so,
Knowing you're going to have a fit,
I've gone over to Gran's to lie low for a bit.

Brian Patten

Rat It Up

C'mon everybody
Slap some grease on those paws
Get some yellow on your teeth
And, uh, sharpen up your claws

There's a whole lot of sausage
We're gonna swallow down
We're going to jump out the sewers
And rock this town

Cos we're ratting it up
Yes we're ratting it up
Well we're ratting it up
For a ratting good time tonight

Ain't got no compass
You don't need no map
Just follow your snout
Hey, watch out for that trap!

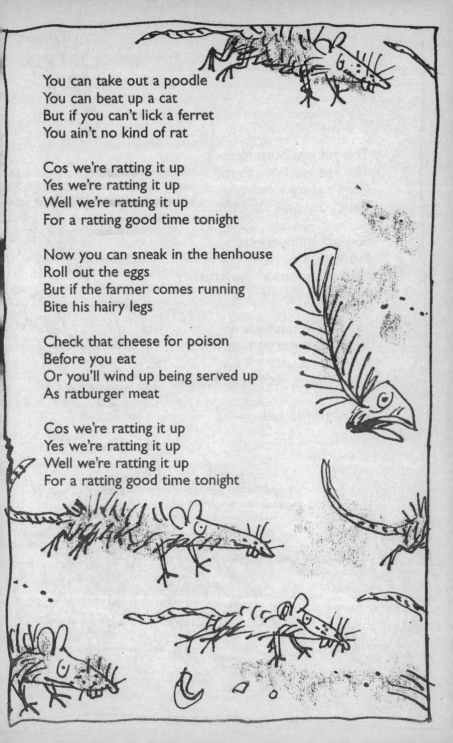

You can take out a poodle
You can beat up a cat
But if you can't lick a ferret
You ain't no kind of rat

Cos we're ratting it up
Yes we're ratting it up
Well we're ratting it up
For a ratting good time tonight

Now you can sneak in the henhouse
Roll out the eggs
But if the farmer comes running
Bite his hairy legs

Check that cheese for poison
Before you eat
Or you'll wind up being served up
As ratburger meat

Cos we're ratting it up
Yes we're ratting it up
Well we're ratting it up
For a ratting good time tonight

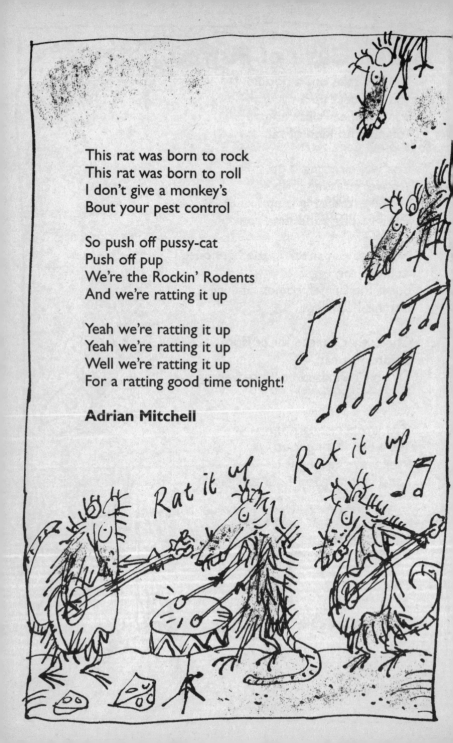

This rat was born to rock
This rat was born to roll
I don't give a monkey's
Bout your pest control

So push off pussy-cat
Push off pup
We're the Rockin' Rodents
And we're ratting it up

Yeah we're ratting it up
Yeah we're ratting it up
Well we're ratting it up
For a ratting good time tonight!

Adrian Mitchell

and smiled

and smiled

and smiled.

Judith Nicholls

Give Yourself a Hug

Give yourself a hug
when you feel unloved

Give yourself a hug
when people put on airs
to make you feel a bug

Give yourself a hug
when everyone seems to give you
a cold-shoulder shrug

Give yourself a hug –
a big big hug

And keep on singing,
'Only one in a million like me
Only one in a million-billion-trillion-zillion
like me.'

Grace Nichols

A Bad Case of Fish

A chip-shop owner's in the dock
on a charge of assault and battery.
The monkfish takes the oath:
So help me Cod . . .

The courtroom's packed with lost soles.
The crabby judge can't find his plaice
or read the prosecution's whiting.
And what sort of fish is a saveloy, anyway?

The young skates are getting bored.
They start skateboarding down the aisles.
The scampi scamper to and fro.
The eels are dancing congers.

But the case is cut and dried.
It's all wrapped up. (Just look
in the evening paper.) Next,
the Krayfish twins . . .

Philip Gross

The Excuse

She walked in nervously, biting her lip;
Trembling slightly, she could not meet their gaze.
'WELL?' shouted the class together –
Startled, the teacher made for the desk where
Behind the relative security of four wooden legs and
A jar of fading daisies
She felt an explanation coming on.
'WHERE'S OUR HOMEWORK?' yelled the class.
'Erm, well,' said the teacher, 'I haven't got it with me.'
'A LIKELY STORY,' sneered the class.
'YOU HAVEN'T DONE IT, HAVE YOU?' chorused the class.
'YOU HAVEN'T EVEN BOTHERED TO MARK OUR
    HOMEWORK!' they cried.
Inside her head she scrabbled desperately for something
    believable,
Sweat trickling down her temple and inside her palms.
'I dropped it getting off the bus. It landed
In a puddle then a
Huge gang of teachers took it off me and said
I wouldn't be let into the Staffroom Coffee-Tea Rotation
    Posse if I did it.
"Marking homework is for wimps," they said,' she said sadly,
A big round tear rolling slowly down her cheek.
'OH,' said the class, shifting uncomfortably,
'WELL, JUST MAKE SURE YOU HAVE IT FOR
    TOMORROW.
THERE, THERE, NO NEED TO CRY.'
'Thank you, class,' sniffed the teacher, brightening a little.
'It won't happen again, I promise.'

Jane Wright

Horace the Horrid

The day that baby Horace hatched
his proud mum gave a ROAR,
then stomped around to show him off
to her monster friends next door.
She named him HORACE THE HORRID –
she was sure he'd be quite a lad –
but soon it was clear, to her horror,
that Horace just wasn't bad.

You're supposed to EAT children, Horace,
not ask them out to play!
You're HORACE THE HORRID, Horace,
PLEASE put that teddy away!

Those feet are for kicking, Horace;
don't hide your claws under the mat!
That playpen's your BREAKFAST, Horace,
You're a MONSTER, remember that!

I'm sorry, said Horace, bowing his head.
I'm sorry to be such a bore,
but I'd rather eat carrots than children
and I really don't know how to roar.
And he carried on humming his quiet hum
till his mother grew quite wild,
but Horace the Horrid just opened his mouth
and smiled and smiled and smiled.
He opened his gummy, grinny mouth

and smiled

and smiled

and smiled.

Judith Nicholls

39

Give Yourself a Hug

Give yourself a hug
when you feel unloved

Give yourself a hug
when people put on airs
to make you feel a bug

Give yourself a hug
when everyone seems to give you
a cold-shoulder shrug

Give yourself a hug –
a big big hug

And keep on singing,
'Only one in a million like me
Only one in a million-billion-trillion-zillion
like me.'

Grace Nichols

41

Cows on the Beach

Two cows,
fed-up with grass, field, farmer,
barged through barbed wire
and found the beach.
Each mooed to each:
This is a better place to be,
a stretch of sand next to the sea,
this is the place for me.
And they stayed there all day,
strayed this way, that way,
over to rocks,
past discarded socks,
ignoring the few people they met
(it wasn't high season yet).
They dipped hooves in the sea,
got wet up to the knee,
they swallowed pebbles and sand,
found them a bit bland,
washed them down with sea-water,
decided they really ought to
rest for an hour.
Both were sure
they'd never leave here.
Imagine, they'd lived so near
and never knew!
With a swapped moo
they sank into sleep,
woke to the yellow jeep

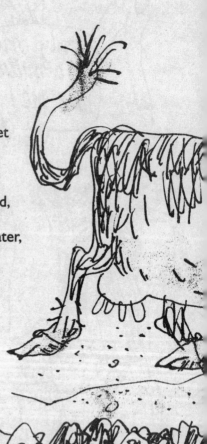

of the farmer
revving there
feet from the incoming sea.
This is no place for cows to be,
he shouted, and slapped them
with seaweed, all the way home.

Matthew Sweeney

Short Visit, Long Stay

The school trip was a special occasion
But we never reached our destination
Instead of the Zoo
I was locked in the loo
On an M62 Service Station.

Paul Cookson

Walking the Dog Seems Like Fun to Me

I said, The dog wants a walk.

Mum said to Dad, It's your turn.
Dad said, I always walk the dog.
Mum said, Well I walked her this morning.
Dad said, She's your dog.
I didn't want a dog in the first place.

Mum said, It's your turn.

Dad stood up and threw the remote control
at the pot plant.
Dad said, I'm going down the pub.
Mum said, Take the dog.

Dad shouted, No way!
Mum shouted, You're going nowhere!

I grabbed Judy's lead
and we both bolted out the back door.

The stars were shining like diamonds.
Judy sniffed at a hedgehog, rolled up in a ball.
She ate a discarded kebab on the pavement.
She tried to chase a cat that ran up a tree.

Walking the dog
seems like fun to me.

Roger Stevens

Victoria's Poem

Send me upstairs without any tea,
refuse me a plaster to stick on my knee.

Make me kiss Grandpa who smells of his pipe,
make me eat beetroot, make me eat tripe.

Throw all my best dolls into the river.
Make me eat bacon and onions – with liver.

Tell Mr Allan I've been a bad girl,
rename me Nellie, rename me Pearl.

But don't, even if
the world suddenly ends,
            ever again,
                Mother,
wipe my face with a tissue
in front of my friends.

Fred Sedgwick

Listn Big Brodda Dread, Na!

My sista is younga than me.
My sista outsmart five-foot three.
My sista is own car repairer
and yu nah catch me doin judo with her.

> I sey I wohn get a complex
> I wohn get a complex.
> Then I see the muscles my sista flex.

My sista is tops at disco dance.
My sista is well into self-reliance.
My sista plays guitar and drums
and wahn see her knock back double rums.

> I sey I wohn get a complex
> I wohn get a complex.
> Then I see the muscles my sista flex.

My sista doesn mind smears of grease and dirt.
My sista'll reduce yu with sheer muscle hurt.
My sista says no guy goin keep her phone-bound –
with own car my sista is a wheel-hound.

> I sey I wohn get a complex
> I wohn get a complex.
> Then I see the muscles my sista flex.

James Berry

The Dragon in the Cellar

There's a dragon!
There's a dragon!
There's a dragon in the cellar!
Yeah, we've got a cellar-dweller.
There's a dragon in the cellar.

He's a cleanliness fanatic,
takes his trousers and his jacket
to the dragon from the attic
who puts powder by the packet
in a pre-set automatic
with a rattle and a racket
that's disturbing and dramatic.

There's a dragon!
There's a dragon!
There's a dragon in the cellar!
with a flame that's red 'n' yeller.
There's the dragon in the cellar . . .

... and a dragon on the roof
who's only partly waterproof,
so she's borrowed an umbrella
from the dragon in the cellar.

There's a dragon!
There's a dragon!
There's a dragon in the cellar!
If you smell a panatella
it's the dragon in the cellar.

And the dragon from the study's
helping out his cellar buddy,
getting wet and soap-suddy
with the dragon from the loo
there to give a hand too,
while the dragon from the porch
supervises with a torch.
Though the dragon from the landing,
through a slight misunderstanding,
is busy paint-stripping and sanding.

There's a dragon!
There's a dragon!
There's a dragon in the cellar!
Find my dad, and tell the feller
there's a dragon in the cellar . . .

 . . . where the dragon from my room
goes zoom, zoom, zoom
in a cloud of polish and spray-perfume,
cos he's the dragon whom
they pay to brighten up the gloom
with a mop and a duster and a broom, broom, broom.

There's a dragon!
There's a dragon!
There's a dragon in the cellar!
Gonna get my mum and tell her
there's a dragon in the cellar.

Nick Toczek

Where Do All The Teachers Go?

Where do all the teachers go
When it's 4 o'clock?
Do they live in houses
And do they wash their socks?

Do they wear pyjamas
And do they watch TV?
And do they pick their noses
The same as you and me?

Do they live with other people
Have they mums and dads?
And were they ever children
And were they ever bad?

weeeee eeeeee ee

Did they ever, never spell right
Did they ever make mistakes?
Were they punished in the corner
If they pinched the chocolate flakes?

Did they ever lose their hymn books
Did they ever leave their greens?
Did they scribble on the desk tops
Did they wear old dirty jeans?

I'll follow one back home today
I'll find out what they do
Then I'll put it in a poem
That they can read to you.

Peter Dixon

No Bread

I wish I'd made a list
I forgot to get the bread.
If I forget it again
I'll be dead.

We had blank and butter pudding,
beans on zip.
Boiled egg with deserters,
no chip butty: just chip.

I wish I'd made a list
I forgot to get the bread.
My mam got the empty bread bin
and wrapped it round my head.

Our jam sarnies were just jam
floating on the air.
We spread butter on the table
cos the bread wasn't there.

My mam says if I run away
she knows I won't be missed,
not like the bread was . . .
I wish I'd made a list!

Ian McMillan

Larks with Sharks

I love to go swimming when a great shark's about,
I tease him by tickling his tail and his snout
With the ostrich's feather I'm never without
And when I start feeling those glinty teeth so close
With a scrunchy snap snap on my ankles or toes
I swim off with a laugh (for everyone knows
An affectionate nip from young sharky just shows
How dearly he loves every bit of his friend),
And when I've no leg just a stumpy chewed end
I forgive him for he doesn't mean to offend;
When he nuzzles my head, he never intends
With his teeth so delightfully set out in rows
To go further than rip off an ear or a nose,
But when a shark's feeling playful, why, anything goes!
With tears in his eyes he'll take hold of my arm
Then twist himself round with such grace and such charm

The bits slip down his throat – no need for alarm!
I've another arm left! He means me no harm!

He'll play stretch and snap with six yards of insides
The rest will wash up on the beach with the tides
What fun we've all had, what a day to remember –
Yes, a shark loves a pal he can slowly dismember.

David Orme

A Dog's Life

I don't like being me sometimes,
    slumped here
on the carpet, cocking my ears
    every time
someone shuffles or shifts their feet,
    thinking
could be going walkies or getting grub
    or allowed to see
if the cat's left more than a smell
    on her plate.
She's never refused, that cat! Sometimes
    I find myself
dreaming (twitching my eyes, my fur)
    of being just
say *half* as canny as her, with her pert miaow,
    her cheeky tail
flaunting! These people sprawled
    in armchairs
gawping at telly, why don't they play ball
    with me
or enjoy a good nose-licking, eh?

Matt Simpson

A Chance in France

'Stay at home,'
Mum said.

But I —
took a chance
in France,
turned grey
for the day
in St Tropez,
I forgot
what I did
in Madrid,
had some tussles
in Brussels
with a trio
from Rio,
lost my way
in Bombay,
nothing wrong
in Hong Kong,
felt calmer
in Palma,
and quite nice
in Nice,
yes, felt finer
in China,
took a room
in Khartoum
and a villa
in Manilla,
had a 'do'

in Peru
with a llama
from Lima,
took a walk
in New York
with a man
from Milan,
lost a sneaker
in Costa Rica
got lumbago
in Tobago,
felt a menace
in Venice,
was a bore
in Singapore,
lost an ear
in Korea,
some weight
in Kuwait,
tried my best
as a guest
in old Bucharest,
got the fleas
in Belize
and came home.

Pie Corbett

Copyright Acknowledgements

All the poems in this collection have first appeared or are shortly to appear in collections published by Macmillan Children's Books. Thanks to the following for the poems which were first published elsewhere:

Matt Simpson for 'A Dog's Life' first published in *The Pig's Thermal Underwear* by Headland Press.

Fred Sedgwick for 'Victoria's Poem' first published in *Blind Date* by Tricky Sam! Publications, Ipswich.

David Harmer for 'Barry's Budgie . . . Beware!' first published in *Spill the Beans* by A Twist In The Tale Press.

Peter Dixon for 'Where Do All the Teachers Go?' first published in *Grow Your Own Poems* by Thomas Nelson.

Gareth Owen for 'Den to Let' from *Salford Road and other poems published* by HarperCollins 1988.

Carol-Ann Duffy for 'Chocoholic'.

Philip Gross for 'A Bad Case Of Fish' first appeared in *The All-Nite Cafe* published by Faber and Faber Ltd.

Ian McMillan for 'No Bread'.

James Berry for 'Listn Big Brodda Dread, Na!' from *When I Dance* © James Berry 1996 first published by Hamish Hamilton Ltd. Reprinted by permission of the Peters Fraser and Dunlop Group Limited on behalf of James Berry.

Grace Nichols for 'Give Yourself A Hug' from *Give Yourself A Hug* reproduced with permission of Curtis Brown Ltd on behalf of Grace Nichols.

Matthew Sweeney for 'Cows on the Beach' first published in *The Flying Spring Onion* by Faber and Faber Ltd.

John Agard for 'Poetry Jump-Up' from *When I Dance* first published by Hamish Hamilton Children's Books.

Adrian Mitchell for 'Rat It Up' from *Balloon Lagoon* published by Orchard Books.

Educational Health Warning! Adrian Mitchell asks that none of his poems are used in connection with any examinations whatsoever.

Brian Patten for 'Dear Mum' from *Thawing Frozen Frogs* first published by the Penguin Group reproduced with permission of the author c/o Rogers, Coleridge and White Ltd.

Roger McGough for 'A Good Poem' from *In The Glassroom* first published by Jonathan Cape. Reprinted by permission of the Peters Fraser and Dunlop Group Limited on behalf of Roger McGough.